TALES OF HORROR
GHOSTS

by Jim Pipe

BEARPORT
PUBLISHING

New York, New York

Credits

Amit Gogia CyberMedia Services: 28–29; Nathan B Dappen: 30–31; Gilles DeCruyenaere: 9; Denisenko: 5R; Fortean Picture Library: 8; Chris Harvey: 7; Image Select: 31; Raymond Kasprzak: 18; Jimmy Lee: 24; Paramount/Everett/Rex Features: 4; Vladimír Radosa: 12–13; Tomek Sikora/The Image Bank/Getty Images: Cover, Title Page; ShutterStock: 5, 10–11, 14, 16–17, 19, 20, 22, 22–23, 26; ticktock Media image archive: 6, 10, 12, 26–27, 28; Clive Watkins: 15; Maria Weidner: 16; Darren Wiseman: 25.

Every effort has been made to trace the copyright holders and we apologize in advance for any unintentional omissions. We would be pleased to insert the appropriate acknowledgment in any subsequent edition of this publication.

Library of Congress Cataloging-in-Publication Data

Pipe, Jim, 1966–
  Ghosts / by Jim Pipe.
     p. cm. — (Tales of horror)
  Includes index.
  ISBN-13: 978-1-59716-203-6 (library binding)
  ISBN-10: 1-59716-203-5 (library binding)
  ISBN-13: 978-1-59716-210-4 (pbk.)
  ISBN-10: 1-59716-210-8 (pbk.)
  1. Ghosts— Juvenile literature. I. Title. II. Series: Pipe, Jim, 1966– Tales of horror.

  BF1461.P55 2007
  133.1— dc22
                              2006013178

For more information, write to Bearport Publishing Company, Inc., 101 Fifth Avenue, Suite 6R, New York, New York 10003. Printed in the United States of America.

10 9 8 7 6 5 4 3 2 1

The Tales of Horror series was originally developed by ticktock Media Ltd.

Table of Contents

Welcome to the Spirit World

Be afraid, be very afraid! Ghosts have been giving people goose bumps for centuries.

Ghosts are said to be restless spirits that cannot find peace in death. They are able to walk through walls and even living people. They may appear in many forms—a horrible face at the window, a **phantom** ship floating above the sea, or a bright ball of light.

Most people don't believe that ghosts exist, but some do. This book presents some of the most chilling **legends** and **lore** surrounding these spooky creatures. Should such stories be taken seriously? Read on and make up your own mind.

Friend or Foe?

According to stories that have been handed down through the ages, ghosts are all around us. Often they do not harm the people who see them. Some good ghosts even try to help strangers stay away from danger.

Be warned, however. There is also a chance of meeting less friendly ghosts. These scary spooks play tricks on people or push them around. Unfortunately, they can appear anywhere, at any time—or so the stories say!

What Is a Ghost?

A ghost is often thought to be the spirit of a person who has stayed on Earth after death. Usually the spirit remains because of unfinished business. Some ghosts want a proper burial. Others want **revenge** on their killers. The ghosts leave only once their business is taken care of.

These troubled spirits have appeared at many times and in many places. Some people say the ghosts they have seen looked like humans. Other people, such as some ghost hunters, believe these spirits are not so easy to see. They think ghosts are just electrical energy left over when people die. So to find them, they use electrical **detectors**.

Ghostly Habits

Ghosts have all sorts of unusual habits, just like people! Some ghosts appear just once. Others keep returning to the same place.
The headless ghost of Anne Boleyn (left) haunts eight different places in England. Perhaps she is still angry at her husband, King Henry VIII. He had her **beheaded** in 1536.

Looking Ghostly

What do ghosts look like? They do not have solid bodies, so people often describe them as being "silvery" or "shadowy." Beyond this common **trait**, however, ghosts can be as different as they were when they were living people.

Some ghosts drag chains behind them. Perhaps they were criminals before they died. Others carry their heads under their arms because they died when their heads were cut off. Still others wear battle **armor** and carry spears. They may have been soldiers in ancient Rome.

Probably the spookiest ghosts are those without eyes. When you look at the face of this kind of ghost, two empty sockets stare back at you!

Ghost Armies

Ghosts are usually lonely figures, but armies of ghosts have often been spotted on battlefields. Some people have even found footprints in the mud left by long-dead soldiers and their horses.

In August 1914, British soldiers were fighting in Belgium. They claimed the ghost of St. George, the traditional protector of England, helped save them—along with an army of phantom **archers**.

9

Haunted Houses

When people think of places where ghosts might appear, they mostly think of haunted houses and castles. One of the most famous examples of a haunted house is in Belmez, Spain.

There, on August 23, 1971, homeowner Maria Pereira caught sight of a mark that looked like a face on her kitchen floor. She tried to scrub it off, but it only grew bigger. The floor was ripped up and replaced. Yet the face appeared again.

Over the years, different faces appeared and disappeared. Finally, the floor was ripped up again. This time the workmen found a graveyard underneath the house!

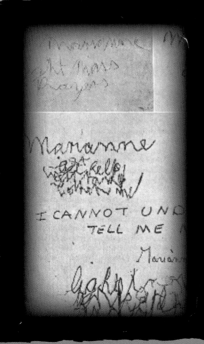

The Most Haunted House?

A famous ghost hunter named Harry Price investigated a house called Borley **Rectory** in the 1930s. It has been called "the most haunted house in England."

Harry found mysterious writing (left) on the walls. He also recorded mysterious footsteps, ringing doorbells, smashed glasses, flying stones, and people being thrown from their beds.

Making Contact

Ghosts get in touch with the living in many different—and frightening—ways. They can spook animals, blow out candles, or make objects suddenly disappear and reappear again. Some ghosts let people know they are present with strange smells. Others can make a room suddenly feel very cold.

Many ghosts make a lot of noise as they make themselves known. They can create the sounds of footsteps, knocking, scratching, bell-ringing, or whispering. Often they shriek and moan. Banshees are Irish ghosts with a scream so sharp it can shatter glass!

Mysterious Music

Some ghosts just can't stop making music. Famous jazz musician Glenn Miller died in a plane crash on December 15, 1944. Ever since, the ghostly sound of his trombone has been heard near the site of his crash in the English Channel.

Poltergeists

CRASH! A plate flies across the room and smashes into the wall. Yet no one is in sight. Then another plate goes flying. What is happening?

The German word *poltergeist* (POHL-tur-gyest) means "noisy ghost." Poltergeists often attach themselves to one place or person. Poltergeists picked on Eleonore Zügun, a 12-year-old Romanian girl, from 1925 to 1927. Stones were thrown against her house by invisible powers. Also, strange forces slapped her and left scratches on her face.

Poltergeists can make objects or even people rise into the air. They also light fires, blow winds through a house, and slam doors. Having a poltergeist around can be a real problem!

Tidy Ghosts

Russian folklore tells of a special kind of poltergeist called a *domovoy*. This household spirit looks like a tiny old man with a face covered in white fur. If people don't look after their homes, the ghost tickles them as they sleep, knocks on the wall, and throws pans and plates.

Ghost Hunters

Most people do not believe in ghosts. All the same, large numbers of ghosts are reported every year. People known as ghost hunters take these **sightings** seriously and investigate them.

In 1851, the Ghost Club Society was founded. It was the first organization to try to record the presence of ghosts. When it was founded, ghost hunters didn't have many tools. They used candles to pick up ghostly breezes. They also sprinkled chalk or flour on surfaces to find ghostly prints.

Today's ghost hunters use hi-tech equipment. Laptop computers are linked to **sensors**. The sensors start cameras that have been set up to catch ghosts on video. Modern ghostbusters also use sensitive thermometers that pick up sudden changes in temperature.

Cat Patrol

In the past, people used cats to detect ghosts. All a cat can do is spit and hiss at a ghost, however. So the cat did not really protect its human companions—but at least people knew the ghost was there!

Well-Known Ghosts

A car drives along a road. Suddenly, a hitchhiker appears at the roadside. The car stops, the hitchhiker climbs in—and later vanishes.

Certain kinds of spirits, such as the phantom hitchhiker, appear often in ghost stories. Usually, the phantom asks the driver for a ride to a place that turns out to be the graveyard where its body is buried!

The "**gallows** ghost" is another popular spirit. Long ago, criminals were hanged from trees near two roads that crossed each other. If the criminal came back as a ghost, people believed that the roads going in four directions would confuse him. The ghost wouldn't know which way to go. So he'd be unable to leave and haunt anyone.

Ghosts of the Famous

Many witnesses have reported seeing the ghosts of famous people. President Abraham Lincoln was **assassinated** in 1865. His ghost is said to haunt the White House in Washington, D.C. In the 1930s, Queen Wilhelmina of the Netherlands was staying there. She heard a knock on her door. When she opened it, there stood Lincoln!

Ghostly Animals

Ghost animals are almost as common as human spirits. More often than not, the animals are former pets. However, other kinds of ghost animals have also been seen. A ghostly monkey still haunts a castle in Scotland. The ghost of a giant wild horse, called the White Devil, gallops through the deserts of the western United States.

The most common ghost animals, however, are black dogs. These beasts often appear to people just before they die. Some of these ghostly hounds have been seen bursting into balls of fire. Black Shuck is a phantom black hound that has long been seen in many parts of England. Sir Arthur Conan Doyle based his famous novel, *The Hound of the Baskervilles*, on him.

Birds of Death

In many countries, ghostly white doves have been seen above the beds of people who were about to die. The sound of birds beating their wings against the windows has also been reported.

In some stories, owl ghosts appear at the window of a house and then disappear. They are also thought to announce a death in the family.

Ghostly Transportation

Many stories tell of ghostly cars, trains, ships, and planes. Often these phantom objects seem to have a life of their own. Many people have reported cars that start up without drivers. Others describe old, rusty trucks that blink their headlights—even though no one is inside!

The most famous of all ghost ships is the *Flying Dutchman*. In 1641, it was sailing around the **Cape** of Good Hope, Africa. Then it began to sink during a fierce storm. The captain cried, "I will get around the Cape even if I have to keep sailing until doomsday." His words came true! This phantom ship has been spotted near the Cape many times over the centuries, bringing bad luck to all who see it.

Phantom Flights

Worldwide, there are stories of ghost planes soaring silently across the night sky. These ghostly planes seem to turn up after tragic air crashes.

In 1972, a jet crashed in the Florida Everglades. Soon after, **eerie** stories started spreading. They told how the ghosts of the pilot and the engineer saved another plane from crashing by warning the crew of danger.

23

Ghosts Around the World

It's a party! People all over the world set aside special days to honor the dead. For a short time, they welcome spooks and spirits into their midst.

In Mexico, ghosts are invited into people's homes during the Day of the Dead festival. People celebrate the dead with colorful skeletons and skulls made from sugar. They also have picnics in graveyards.

In ancient Europe, people believed that All Hallow's Eve (October 31) was a night when dead spirits left their graves and wandered the earth. Today, children across the United States and in parts of Europe celebrate Halloween by dressing up and shouting "Trick or treat!"

The Hungry Ghost Festival

The Chinese believe that the dead return to the world of the living once a year. During the Hungry Ghost festival, ghosts wander the earth in search of food. Families offer meals to bring themselves good luck. They burn paper models of objects such as houses, cars, and TV sets. They believe that these items will help the ghosts live comfortably in the spirit world. People also burn fake money, so that ghosts will have more cash to spend there!

Spooky Books

Even people who don't really believe in ghosts enjoy reading about them. The Harry Potter books by J. K. Rowling are full of ghostly characters. They are also some of the best-selling children's books of all time.

Harry Potter goes to a school named Hogwarts, which is haunted by over 20 ghosts. These spirits include Nearly Headless Nick, the grim Bloody **Baron**, and the jolly Fat Friar. A ghost named Myrtle sometimes gets flushed out of the castle in the toilet! These ghosts enjoy a Deathday Party on the anniversaries of their deaths.

More Terrifying Tales

Many other famous books also feature ghosts. Phantom beings often appear in the Goosebumps horror series written by R. L. Stine. In Charles Dickens's *A Christmas Carol*, three different ghosts visit the miserable Scrooge. They encourage him to be more generous and enjoy life.

Movie Ghosts

Ghost movies have been scaring people for more than 100 years. The first horror movie was Georges Méliès's *The Haunted Castle*, made in 1896. Méliès used trapdoors and mirrors to make his ghosts float and vanish.

Since then, **special effects** have come a long way. Spooky faces appear in walls. See-through ghosts zip through the air. Invisible poltergeists send objects flying. As you can see from this photo, *Ghostbusters* (1984) made the most of high-tech special effects. Some other ghost movies that have featured eye-popping special effects are *Beetlejuice* (1988), *Casper* (1995), and *Scooby-Doo* (2002).

Good or Bad Spirits?

Some ghost movies, such as *Casper* (1995), are about friendly spirits. Despite being a ghost, Casper tries to make friends with people.

Most movie ghosts, however, are mean and try to harm people. In *Sleepy Hollow* (1999), a headless horseman races through the countryside, terrifying anyone who dares to come out at night.

Do Ghosts Exist?

People have been claiming to see ghosts for hundreds of years. Yet no one has ever been able to really prove that they exist. So how can all the spooky sightings be explained?

Most ghosts are probably just tricks of the mind. Tired minds can mix up real life and dreams. After all, it's easy to see strange things in the dark.

Other ghosts are the result of dishonest tricks. Often, people claiming to speak to spirits are really looking for money or fame.

Perhaps the main reason that ghosts have been around for so long is that they haunt our imaginations. We simply enjoy feeling scared every now and then.

Fake Photos

Many ghost hunters claim they have taken photographs of ghosts. However, many of these photos have been proven to be fakes.

For example, when two shots are taken using the same piece of film, the two images sit on top of each other. This trick is called a double exposure. It makes people look shadowy and ghost-like. So anyone with the right kind of camera can catch a "ghost" on film!

Glossary

archers (AR-churz) people who shoot arrows with a bow

armor (AR-mur) a metal covering that protects a soldier's body in battle

assassinated (uh-SASS-uh-nate-id) murdered

baron (BA-ruhn) a title given to a powerful person

beheaded (bi-HED-id) had one's head cut off

cape (KAPE) a point of land that sticks out into the sea

detectors (di-TEKT-urz) machines that find or warn of certain things, such as ghosts

eerie (IHR-ee) mysterious, strange

gallows (GAL-ohz) a wooden structure from which criminals are hanged

legends (LEJ-uhnds) stories that have been handed down for a long time

lore (LOR) a collection of traditional stories about a topic

phantom (FAN-tuhm) a ghost or spirit

rectory (REK-tuh-ree) the home of a priest or other religious leader

revenge (ri-VENJ) punishment for something that has been unfairly done

sensors (SEN-surz) devices that note the presence of something; detectors

sightings (SITE-ings) occasions when something is seen

special effects (SPESH-uhl uh-FEKTS) exciting images or sounds in movies, usually produced by technical tricks

trait (TRATE) characteristic

Index